A Day This Lit

A Day This Lit

— POEMS —

Howard Levy

CavanKerry ◈ Press LTD.

FORT LEE, NEW JERSEY

Library of Congress Cataloging-in-Publication Data

Levy, Howard S.

    A day this lit / Howard Levy.

        p. cm.

     ISBN 0-9678856-1-2

      I. Title.

PS3562.E927175 D39 2000

811'.54—dc21   00-035846

Cover Photograph: *Untitled #37* from the *Cape Cod Series* by Harry Callahan, Estate of Harry Callahan, courtesy Pace/MacGill Gallery, New York

Cover and text design by Charles Casey Martin

FIRST EDITION

For Susan, Sam, and Nate

CONTENTS

III

FOREWORD

I once had a neighbor who was fond of the expression "Not so fast." Although he was a plumber rather than a poet, his words always have seemed apt in regard to poetry: poems cannot be in a hurry. Each syllable, as it insists on its physical integrity as a sound, wishes to resist momentum. Yet, as much as poems are the products of concentration and attention, they are also thrill seekers. They live for the tremor of feeling. The trick is that the thrill must not be fast. The exhilaration that is communicated is not dizzying or automotive or giddy. It is delicious and astute and obliquely candid. It makes no claims because its magic suspends all mere reasons. The poems of Howard Levy speak for poetry in this most crucial of ways: they linger precipitously. They tend not to be long poems and their subjects vary from a scene in the South during a voting registration drive in the '60s to Mozart quintets. Sometimes they narrate events and many times they posit an imagistic and metaphorical story line. In all cases, what is striking is how much they render in not much space. Each line of each poem is very carefully joined much as a piece of furniture is pegged together rather than nailed or tacked. The sensibility at work in the poems is a blend of classical decorum — lines obeying the pauses of syntax — and objectivist legerity — lines challenging patterns and emphasizing breath.

The legerity is to be insisted upon because the poems are consistently delightful. I mean this not so much in the sense of amusing (though some are droll) as in the sense of fully engaging our spirits. Because of the economy of his language the reader listens to the poet very carefully. Over and over again the word choices have the quality that is uniquely poetry's: they surprise yet they seem utterly apposite.

The emotional note that impresses the most in these poems is their frank tenderness. The affinity Levy shows for Mozart is perhaps the most captivating instance of this tenderness. Levy's evocations of Mozart's musical pieces and his life and times are uncanny in their ability to portray in words the gift of feelings that reside in the world of pure sound. Yet the poems about Mozart are a good deal more than diminuendo fireworks; they convey most movingly the humanity of Mozart. Indeed, the most ambitious poems, such as "Three Letters," "Overture from *Cosi Fan Tutte*," and "An Answer" present the reader with a feeling of the enormous soulfulness, joy and vulnerability that distinguish Mozart's achievement. This is a remarkable imaginative accomplishment. Our being human tends either to be taken for granted or puffed up. For his part, Levy can segue in the course of three poems from Kabbalism to "Joe Adcock, Power Hitter of the Braves" to some letters from Mozart to Haydn. The common note threading the poems is an unashamed humanity, a willingness to look scrupulously and yet rejoice in the small and large mysteries. The book represents an oeuvre that has evolved over patient decades. Art takes its time because it knows how long the odds are against our achieving anything that has the strength of beauty. This book has poems that are keepers, poems that can look in the face of time without flinching.

— *Baron Wormser*

…and the dark released a few hostages.
— William Matthews

I

This Web

You knew how things open,
a flower, a jail, an eye
and at the very last, a hand.

It is already evening when the hand
opens. The streetlights have come on,
people absorbed into their coats
and scarves hurry along the street.
No one speaks, not many even
look around them, they spare themselves
the torments of community.

In a small restaurant off the Central Square,
the first diners of the evening have entered.
A waiter who only this morning dreamed
of the exhaustion of his charity rises.
As he stands over them, you write —
their hands poised to eat, his poised
to serve, the cook's to cook —

this intimate whisper of revelation:
this web of hands.

in honor of Aleksander Wat

3

A Poem about Furniture

Maybe it is 3 A.M., maybe it is a dank
and drear November afternoon,
a thin orphan's porridge of light
in an always darkened, empty room.

First question: does the furniture wait?
The psychological question, cousin
to the tree falls in the forest,
in this silly age, a question of network
and dependency. Does the chair
understand itself in terms of seatings,
is it haunted through these empty hours
by its need for function, its dread
of the plush velvet of potential?
Or does it stand on its own legs?

And the second: do the pieces of furniture
talk among themselves? The Nutcracker question,
our sense of the renegade life,
the truth just outside the door, what
lies submerged under the tide's last inch,
the whole roster of being, that which we dream on
and count on to be there, but is incalculable.

Third: if they talk,
what do they talk about? This is the political question,

rising from the fears of the imperialists,
the terrors of the slaveowners. What is going on
down in the cabins, do they plot or do they sing?
It means, how exposed are our weaknesses, how imposing
our shame and guilt.

Fourth: what is their language?
The philosophical question, how do we imagine
a grammar of the intransitive world?
What is its necessary order, what
modifies what?

While the final question reverts to us:
what is it here, these chairs and desks, a sofa,
the silence of arrangement, that so
compels us? What part of us
is mirrored here: the calm, the dead
or its burning opposite: the need toward life?

The dialectic of purity, so that what lurks here
might just be the sacred: a community of believers,
a brethren in the darkness and matins,
the rising of voices toward the votive of dawn,
the celebration by all that waits, by all
that, singing, may reach and connect.

for Baron Wormser

Jackson, Mississippi, 1966

When she suddenly said "Jump," holding on
to the old woman's hand, not letting go at all
though the woman was anxious to get away
from us, the trouble we brought, the mixing up
of settled things, the warm February air
of Mississippi seemed to me to collaborate,
to sustain our white college boy
arms and heads higher and longer than possible.

Mrs. Carolyn Williams, two hundred pounds if a one,
just back to her native Jackson
after the poison of Chicago, grown huge
with her appetite for change, knew
this one would never register to vote,
70, a retarded daughter in tow, scared
even by a knock at her door,
one Negro woman, two white men,
since white folks on her dirt street only meant pain
or viciousness, the bill collectors or the police,
but still deserved a treat, a gift of a moment from the future
and a joke on the rotted past.

And so when the old woman asked which of the two white men
was in charge, Mrs. Williams just turned to us
and commanded "Jump" and we jumped:
the Red Sea didn't part, the Confederate

flag didn't come down from the gold-domed Capitol
and what changed was just enough in the woman's eyes
and Mrs. Williams released her.

for Shaun Griffin

Hands

(How to hold her, or this moment)
The silence falls most heavily on the hands.

A species of genius and a species of fish,
the elegant and wise floating through the air,
a combination of propulsion and density,
but more is how they affect us, teach us
of the sadness of touch without words.
All they know tapped on a desk
or slid along a cheek, and so
movies in the dark that we grow grateful for,
because they can rest
and each thing we know is impersonal.

I Enter Brooklyn
through the Rashomon Gate

The rain pours and each story can amaze.

A warm, close September night, sitting on the porch
with my father and my uncle, my mother
and aunt moving through the lighted windows,
the Dodgers on the radio beating the Braves,
the pennant and Newcombe looking good,
and later after the game, chocolate ices
in their ribbed white paper cups,
each thing glowing in its expected place.

But what did I know of their lives,
their money troubles, their sex troubles,
their losses, their violence?
What could I have understood of the story
of the other woman or the other man,
how could I have listened to it
and how could it have been told to me?

I squat over the fire,
self as storyteller,
rain drenching the memory,
washing the last skin of innocence
down the unfathomable, unbearable street.

A Bad Day

The soul is a building,
not a home.

Red brick, two stories,
built for small industrial use
in a neighborhood without amenities
and you approach it,
that is, your own, always from the back.
From that way, the only details
are the gates on the windows.

A '72 Chevy, its paint
barely holding any color,
the front bumper hanging off on the right,
sits parked at the side of the building
every time you look.

You don't know why it's there,
and you don't know, most of all,
to whom it belongs.

Matisse in the Rotogravure: The Cutouts

He calls the scissors "neighbor,"
they have lived next to him for twenty years.
He laughs, I admire their garden and their children,
it amazes me how sharp steel
can make things grow.

Age, he says, is just another color,
one, frankly, he would prefer not to use.

Do you know my goal? he asks.
Heraclitus, he says. I do not ever
want to step in the same light twice.

What We Ask For

Great granaries of sunlight,
doors flung open,
everything for a gracious asking and taking,
everything orderly, people quiet and amused on line,
convinced and calm that there is more than enough

or the fjord ice-blocked.
White except for a slice of a pine's deep green
toward the east, the smoke from the cabin's chimney
the sheerest of greys.
A man and a woman drink tea
by the window. They have loved each other
for less than a week
and that is where in the scene we find
the voluminous red of the bougainvillea.

The Adoration

In this *Adoration*, possibly Lippi,
a small angel, far on the right,
in a bliss profound and active,
begins slowly to rise, to ascend
to its source.

It is unwilling to leave the Child
and maybe one beat of its wings
will settle it back, or contemplation
of the Child's skin, the exact texture
of the ultimate miracle,

will anchor it to the scene.
But the centuries have worn on it,
the gold of its halo has abraded,
worn down to disks amid the red
clay bole, and the gesso has chipped,

flaked, leaked from the panel,
the gold leaf with it.
Do angels go in for repairs?
Do their wings sometime slide
out of alignment?

I know a woman, who, as she left,
in this flat end of a country,

in this night so stupidly dark,
so filled with the imprecision
of men and women crossing their lives

and thus a marriage broken,
sons too far away and the future
too close, seemed to hold
a small cup of light around her.
Is it too much to compare her to an angel?

No. Because what I saw, her figure
diminishing in the blackened bole,
was what I believe,
love and its joy of intervention,
its sudden annunciation.

Lovers

They fall out of the sky.

We try to credit some inspired smile
but the truth is they fall out of the sky.

The truth is we have our beds on wheels,
we roll around the city
tuned to the weather channel.

They fall out of the sky, exactly
as we remember or forget,
the unprepared but predominating fact,

and into our laps,
they fall into our shrieking laps.

The Vibrant Archipelagoes

Two sailors deepening their drunk at the bar,
rattan, the steams of these islands,
palm trees and palm trees,
palms around a glass. Conrad's
been dead for seventy years now
and inside I've finally come to my novel
of the equator, the vibrant archipelagoes,
the dreams coming from the furnaces,
the sailors inside those dreams.

The heat rises in the morning
and everything inflicts its color,
the gargantuan yellows and purples
of toucans, the spilled
scarlet of macaws, the sea's
connected twins of blue and green,
this world so amorally grown,
so unearned, that relief comes
as the cloudy brown of whiskey,
the fog of slurred speech,
unnameable identities of driftwood,
the world curdled, loss and limits added,
filtered into the daily blazings of light.

The quiet of a manuscript.
 In the library, under glass,
stable in the special light,
early drafts and typescripts of *The Secret Sharer*
and *The Heart of Darkness*. Marlow,
compressed to a voice, here compressed to ink,
the great rivers flowing in these curls
of blue and black, heat and light
and flesh flattened into scrawls.

And the drone of ambition.
Where is my tale, my telling,
my island, the rain that suddenly floods,
the clouds black as goddess' hair?

Like pollen grains on an orchid,
the ship waits an anchor.
Out through the breakers they row
swollen with destinations. The boat,
the South China Sea, Goa, Cape Town,
swinging up the Atlantic,
Dakar, Gibraltar, Cardiff.
One dreams of a small coal freighter
to Bergen. The fjords, the cold grey skies,
the decency of soft rain, propriety of snow.
The other thinks he will take his rest
in Wales. Maybe mine, maybe farm
the sullen land. He will dig, he thinks,
lingering over the syllable.

And yet the storm will come,
the main mast will shiver,
the mizzen will crack.
I will give them the foamy swirls
of shipwreck, rafts of floating deck,
the decreasing chance of rescue,
waterless days and the sudden white
of sails bearing toward them.

At Orlestone, on his desk,
neat piles of chapters like the risen
archipelagoes of his languages:
Polish, German, French, English.

He stands at the window,
studies his garden. Rocket
and phlox, larkspur, the good
soldiers of hedge, and in the corner
on wooden stalks painted green,
he has planted three drawings of *Arachnis*,
the spider orchid of Malaya, its petals
long yellow tongues dripped with red.

He wonders what he will have to answer for,
but in the meanwhile gives Marlow a beard,
shaves Marlow's face.

II

The Kabbalist's Pencil

The pencil that had found silence and become silence
and must not name the name of silence.

Gnostic at dawn, gnostic at noon
and at dusk, a startle of ducks rise from the marshgrass.

Can metal or the knocking of the woodpecker
heal us? Our reflections in a mirror?

Always, blessed be, as a mother
outside the school, is the dream waiting

Though the dream is without deeds,
the dream is without hands.

Who has picked up the ripened fruit
after it has fallen from the tree? Who

After Adam, after Eve,
has not learned from its taste?

Who has not written through the day
and read their words into an unforgiving night,

With the light seeming banished,
and not despaired for dawn

Rising over the forest, rising over the house,
over the chimney smoke that gives black its earnest name?

And so who will climb the ladder, hand over hand,
with the pencil more bold than the prayer it writes?

1958

Early that year, Leslie Bloom got leukemia
and that summer, many nights
I would awaken and throw up.
I held a fear and grief so central
I would retch to the driest of heaves
yet leave it untouched.
I was terrified by the betrayals
of the blood, and it got so
I needed to chant myself to sleep,
chanting the title of an article
just out in *Sport* magazine:
"Joe Adcock, Power Hitter of the Braves."

Joe Adcock, Power Hitter of the Braves.
Joe Adcock, Power Hitter of the Braves.
After all, I was eleven, the factories
of my hormones just gearing up,
running their first test batches
off of the line, and I was innocent
of double meanings, unkissed
by symbol and pun.

That such a clumsy thing gave relief,
adding cock and power and bravery,
that the first simple zing of sex
could start me sleeping, white cells quiet,

grief in bounds, and the clue
of something waiting in the wings
and worth the wait.

Three Letters

1

To my dear friend Haydn,

For the last weeks, I have thought to compose
a music of the misconstrued. An odd idea,
perhaps one of those paradoxes,
as when you awaken
on one of those fiercely bright winter mornings
and stand at your window
alive with the brilliant blue of the tiling
below the window across the street,
sharpened by the diamond glitter
of the small, fresh snow that has fallen overnight,
but yet are drawn most powerfully
to stare at the dull steam rising
from the horses' nostrils.

I think you may be smiling now
imagining your remonstrance:
this is not paradox, but multiplicity,
our talent for expansion,
for filling in every color, every
space and interplay between the tones,
as you have often commanded "Orchestra!"
meaning, enrich the sound.

25

But, maestro,
I mean something more,
I mean something of the failure of beauty
and even the failure of truth
to sometimes convince us.
Do you remember the story of Cassandra,
the clear lines of her sight and her vision
unheeded. I imagine those lines turning to snakes
in her eyes, and what would that music sound like?

And, too, I mean something of its opposite,
the empty music that the crowd believes,
the pretty picture, the anticipated note,
the banality of dukes and duchesses
with their livery of senseless applause,
and I want to search out another music,
not just deeper, richer (yours will always do
for that) but something different in its core,
the harmonics, perhaps, of confusion.

Maestro, this question may be absurd,
but if order is beauty or beauty, order
and both are timeless, if even agony
contains a sense of calm, a way
of its own being,
what is it I feel that looms so
in the drama of the misheard and the missaid?

I think of hesitancies, the rhythm of the stammer,
the flood of voice dammed, all the tones brewing
in that pause as completed as a circle. I think
of the garbled, mumbled declaration of love,
the aside, the whispered, not out of shyness
or gestures of decorum, but out of strangulation,
the deficiency of breath (or courage). Is there
something hidden, something immense and hidden
there? And is it a cello, or possibly a woodwind?

And how to extract it,
find the major of disorder?
I know there is no pause in His plan,
that the light shines unstopping from the sun,
that harmony emanates in unbroken emanation,
and so we have no theory,
no patterns for the unpatterned,
like the randomness of clouds filling the sky.

My dear friend, we both believe in the unbroken light
and our art details it. This is not a loss of faith,
in fact, I am one of those Spanish friars
off to the New World, Christ in my eyes,
in my heart, assured that the uncharted
only waits. But I am drawn to this rent,
to compose the truth of the torn fabric.
How I have gone on, I pray you excuse me,

27

but who else could understand? I remain
with all my heart, dearest friend,
your most sincere friend.

W. A. Mozart

2

My dear Haydn,

It has been two months since my last letter
and Stadler mentioned yesterday you are readying
for London. Did you find what I last said
irregular, quixotic, those large adjectives of the failed?
Or is it new, possibly a footfall
into some sort of amazed continent?

Maestro, I have been consumed with this music,
the first that I do not effortlessly hear. It is
as if music were a city I'd always lived in
and knew every house and every citizen,
each of their rooms and each of their talents,
but one day come upon a street, unnamed,
all the houses locked, all the windows shuttered.
Not one person on the street and I resolve to wait
for someone to arrive to tell me
not only what is here, but more
how I have missed it.

And since no one has come,
I have broken into the houses.
Inside, nothing irregular, acceptable furniture in place,
ashes in the grate, that is, it is not difficult
to make the sounds discordant, the tempos all askew,
but as I wrote, I came to hear and understand it

as one step toward something else,

that confusion is a pause,

as that moment when you enter the darkened room

and move slowly toward the candles to be lit,

and then a door

to the inward silence,

which is like a Chinese box,

its own series of doors,

each one smaller, tighter, each one locked.

Do you see where I am heading?

Not to London unfortunately, but toward a music

of the purest compression,

of the eternal unsaid,

what the heart stands despairingly and perpetually

dumbly in front of.

Imagine the harmonies possible in that music,

imagine the adagios that close that wound.

I thank God that you will understand me

and I remain your most humble and respectful friend.

W. A. Mozart

3

To my dear friend Haydn,

You answer that my questions
intrigue you, that they have returned you
to certain movements that as you put it
always "sounded with silence."
Yes, exactly, there are passages of yours resolute
with silence, not the obvious
sudden absence of wind through the pines,
but silence's active body,
arms, legs, contours of the chest,
the caverns of a singer's body
shaping out her sound.

Maestro, is not that silence an emissary,
a spore, a bud of death
or possibly its opposite,
the residue of all that came before,
all time previous?

I know you are shaking your head,
what gnawing darkness has gotten into you,
my prankish Mozart, and I hear you saying,
music is the carriage of the soul,
roads well laid out, signposts and inns
to the Principality of Beauty,
the Kingdom of Eternal Truth.

It is as indifferent to death
as we are to weather in a distant country.

No, do not mistake me. This is not despair,
the indulgent lounging in the darkness
of the grave, but boldness and ambition,
a call to descend and then return,
to be Aeneas, ancestor of a new Rome,
a new music that we sing
on our walk to the boundaries of His plan.

I know you will send me off with the best of wishes
and your best respects to whomever I find there.

Your most sincere and devoted,
excited and fearful friend.

W. A. Mozart

Reshapings

The shape of your womb
is how I learned to tilt my head
when listening hard, when taking in.
Your legs, one slightly shorter
than the other (not enough to limp
but enough to sculpt the muscles
of your back and tense your walk),
took me through my first merengue,
taught those small refinements
of sway and balance
and life spread over me
simply, cell by new cell,
as light spreads over a shadow,
lessons of pace,
lessons of patience.

*

A dream that you are talking.
You hold a peach and tell me
about the luxuries of shopgirls.
1943. Lord & Taylor, the lingerie
and nylon counter. Twenty,
no soldier to worry over yet plenty
to meet, the jewelry of the jitterbug
and free to stay in the city overnight.

You phrase it, the shiny black satin
of becoming a woman.

*

How quiet we are, the two of us.
Each reading in our favorite
chairs, the rainy afternoon
moving toward dusk and
the making of dinner.
I am proud to chop the onions
and peel the eggs.
I will earn a small piece of cake,
though not enough to ruin my appetite.
How the afternoon we made
enclosed us.

*

And yet such a loneliness chipped at you,
such a bleakness, as if everything
were too narrow,
people, ease, and the coronation
of desire, so that each day the loneliness
broke off some small edge of self
until the small, ruined abbey
of your heart lost its body's faithful.

*

In the hospital,
your legs elephantine with water
growing larger into your death
and my father and I
growing smaller and smaller,
unable to talk directly and honestly to you,
as if you were not
a dying woman
we both loved.

*

This first deep cold day of winter,
the air with no sense of forgiveness.
I clear some last leaves from your grave.
In a few weeks, it will be seven years.
Your grandsons are growing well.

It is so cold, and here in this cemetery,
I imagine that you bear me
once again toward the vastness of future,
while I remember and bear you back
into this tiny present, this brief
regency of noise and light.

Sagaponack

In all the world's blue restlessness,
green restlessness, in all the colors
that itch and slide through our eyes
in this daylight spread like a skirt,
in all the heat-disturbed compasses
of the horizon line, how do we reach?

Today is a day of assembling,
accreting, ingesting the layers
of brilliance and haze, the textures
of pebble and foam, the rigors
and twists of the grass' cellulose,
the startling rococo of a simple beach.

(Entranced by the silence
of desks and pencils in their cups,
of the angled light of lamps
that make edges seem profound,
of the whole curious room
before I entered and after I left,
I have been too thin, spare)

and I see myself, though not without
fear, strafing with the gulls,
with their eyes and their dives
that slice silver from the sea.

Insomnia

The depth of the water rises.
3 A.M. is an hour blacker and muddier
than 2, and by 4, he will be submerged,
two fathoms down.

He damns the soundlessness
of a full house, twelve sleepers, curled
and sprawled, devoted to their beds.
He whispers each of their names,
then describes each of the faces.
He tries to rise on that scaffolding of facts.

But then comes the bends, when the terrible
pressure buries bubbles in the heart,
when what rises over the horizon
is not the sun, but the round, brilliant, blazing
ball of panic, center of the universe.

Cézanne's Fruit

How could you lift them?

The very awkward truth of these apples and pears
that have ripened without sap, that speak
nothing of flowers and the magnanimity of water.
A fruit without weight, without rot,
cast over a mussed white linen
on a table falling or seeming to fall forward
(yet stopped, as if gravity were a choice,
something it could elect to avoid),
they come from the orchard
of the mind's yellow and delicate pollens.

In a letter, he wrote that nothing
in nature (the beautiful bowl of shore
of L'Estaque, the sun already high
and shining over Mont St. Victoire,
the black green forests at Pontoise)
made him want to paint.
Only seeing painting drove him to the work.

The Spanish Poets

With the Spanish poets, the fierce hand
grabs the mantilla and they name it
the sun's blossom.

They say: the air feeds on the scents
of coins, the moon
passes the night whispering
this rock was once a bishop
and the black of the night
is the black eye of Eva,
the black of the corner
the black hair of her arms.

Fear dies in their mouths
because the tongue works the field,
because the teeth are the stray cats
of the plaza, because the world sounds
with birdsong, the poem's only daughter,
the love of his life.

for David Ungar

Early Morning Song

In a fog this thick, I must count
on my fingers — eight days from you.
Everything has folded into fog,
as in Sung paintings
where the accidental details
of the world are lost
and the only clear thing
is The Way.

Each day here has grown hotter.
Yesterday afternoon, charred
by both heat and absence,
I sat still on the porch and tried
to write you a letter. Just too hot,
and someone came along who knew
a waterfall. The lesson is:
how often we get rescued.

I wrote once, as a son,
of fathers and sons,
silence as a medium of exchange,
loss compounded like interest,
the inevitable crash of laissez-faire,
but for you two asleep,

cradling your dreams,
I write something different:

true paths shine in the fog.

for Sam and Nathaniel

Strange Town

Darkness comes with a cooling breeze
and you sit alone, aware of your skin
and your desires,
as simple as getting back home,
as mundane as a sweater.
You cross your arms, hand on elbow,
tighten in

and wit disappears. What replaces it
is a concentration in the eyes,
a small narrowing of the lids, as if
there were something very important
to be seen, only you have been lax.

This is just the old self-betrayal,
that searching you see nothing,
not the park in front of you, the houses
on the hill slowly being lit, and not even
that you are here and that the man
who walks across the street
sees you, the bench, the park
and may be pleased with his night.

And when it is time to be moving,
you will say to yourself,
after all, I have the model of the man

out strolling his town, turning
corners as he likes,
who comes upon me in his scene
and fits me in, flourishing and ordinary.

Polish Prism

In the scuttlebutt of Warsaw
someone is always running into a wall
while the night throws powerful stencils of the crash,
and the trees, lounging, leap to attention at the noise.
This is their contribution
to the need for seriousness.

Meanwhile, an army officer
outflanks the reticence of a maid.
He unbuttons her blouse, she imagines doves.
He cups her breasts, she imagines
the long bus ride back to her distant province.
A merchant in the building next door tallies
his books. They are an atlas
of bankruptcy, the numbers attack him
like swarms of red bees.

What can be said of ruin,
whether fanciful or factual?
Toward what dark churches do the poets go
to attend that litany,
to learn how many candles they need light
when the mind can sufficiently plot
the decaying orbitals of history
and yet the eye, relishing independence,
wanders into restaurants

and signals for sausage, for the strongest
vodka.

in memory of Zbigniew Herbert

Turning Fifty

The role of the evening
has grown so large, so visible
along the street, dead of quiet.
All the porches have stopped breathing,
the windows of the third floor attics without pulse,
a tricycle tipped over on the lawn
in rigor mortis.

I've decided against nostalgia,
as if there had been years of twelve-month summers,
the screen doors' inside/outside alchemy,
diving into lakes with crystal bottoms,
of looks so completely understood
in light so completely trustworthy.

I've decided against fact,
its blatant arithmetic,
the black-edge outline,
certainty as arrogant
as the upper, upper classes.

The moon rises like steam off tea
infusing the evening,
and I decide for shadow,
the hulking of trees, the looming of houses

and the almost life
that you can hear if you are still,

the almost life,
the gush of its watefalls,
the beat of spring run off.

for Susan

Notes on the Neo-Classic

It was not so much the weather,
clouds arriving like uncles and aunts
and the sun disappearing
like a cat through a fence,
though by then I had learned
the chancy strength of atmospherics,
rows upon rows of shade trees
and nothing dappled, a painterly
road full grey in the dishwater light,
and that while the Lord might work
in mysterious ways, loss
does not, transparent along the cheek
and mouth, engraved in the eye.

It was the logic of language,
the austerities of conjugation,
the fixative of agreement
and the delicate permanence
in such a fluid world
of the imperfect tense,
she has left…

Brownian Motion

When we might have been, at last, ourselves,
qualifying that with whatever
we could get away with, weather, architecture,
capacities for bliss and rage, the way
a face naturally set to glumness or farce,
we moved among each other, our
Brownian motion equal parts longing
and the desire to long. Yet
we still could not keep from our study
of infinite gradations, the parsing of look
and gesture, the pauses available
to the terrifically frightened.

You once said that we were the first pair ever
to whom the moon had nothing to say,
and felt wounded by that. I countered,
hours later, that the moon had never said
anything to anybody and you grew filled
with my mistakenness, so filled
that you felt suddenly contented, while the moon
continued on its way, rinsing the fields,
the porch we sat on, and we
accelerated toward dawn.

The Poem

The poem says goodbye to the last guest
and begins to clean up.

The poem put out the food
chose the music

danced the night away
with its favorite.

The poem
had a great success

but is dead tired
and craves it bed

the soft s's and the round double l's
of drifting off to sleep

the long o of the dream
that has flown in from Kyoto

Kyoto of eight hundred years ago
where laugh the most perfect of women

with their blackest
of teeth.

III

Sameness

The fog rolls in from the east
as if some arbitrator ruled
straight down the middle,
an indecipherable fifty-fifty: sea
into sky into sea.

And someone says soup
and another says
how tired and inexact,
if this is minestrone, where are
the vegetables, the pasta
floating by? How about
chicken noodle?

A third shouts
the sun is a matzo ball as yet unladled
as if he were a kamikaze,
and the fourth, tired of the rest
says, all right, puree

which suggests a blender,
God's great Cuisinart and brings a sudden, soft,
graciously freeing moment of clarity:

I am an ingredient.

for William Matthews

Montauk and the World Revealed through the Magic of New Orleans

In the afternoon, a jazz band
of thunderheads rolled in
playing "When the Saints"
so the ocean knew it was funeral
and commenced to lament and dance
and fan itself in the hot day,
the gulls too set to dancing
that quick step they are famous for
(and always do for the tourists)
and then the beach grass, never footloose,
began to clap out the rhythm
and shout
O this is some world
hot city, hot blooming

The Doctor

After days of healing,
he would get away to fish.
Curator of fluff and feathers,
he tied his own flies,
designed his own waders
and up to the lake country
for trout and walleye.

I would ask him, what is it
out there on the water,
and he would say, all week
I swim lead for my school of patients,
take this, take that,
don't eat this, don't eat that,
I tell them swim away from the hook,
don't take that bait, that bug there
has sharp metal innards,
that worm glints steel,
but we are such dumb fish,
such sorry things that we all get pulled
from our lives.
So, weekends,
I choose to be the redresser of balances.

I know that he hid behind this facile
diagnosis because I went with him once

and as we stood thigh-deep
in the cold and clear lake,
he began his meticulous detailings,
the striations of the bottom rocks
and how each different sediment
reflects the light, the distribution
of firs along the shore,
the speckling of the speckled trout
and each thing, he said,
is a symptom and so a clue
into the fevered chemistry of beauty.

Wellfleet

When you find the sea that is marrow to you —
it is always the slate sea, frigid,
divorced from glamor, the sporadic
spiders of whitecaps and indifferent to the sky's
grey, mimicking clouds, then you know
it is mercy that you don't expect

and don't require. The shore
is freezing, but the volume
of steadiness, the quiet, suffusing roar holds you.
And so does the gull
with its ridiculous legs but its direct black eye.

for Phyllis Meadow

What Difference

After a v of geese crosses the sky,
there is a yearning for geese.
He sits on the hood of his car, restless,
crazy to tune himself in
to the Southern Migration,
the great circle of movement.
Through the cut in the dunes,
he watches the ocean kicking up
(a storm approaching from the south),
waves going irregular, crowding
each other, backsplashing.

To take part. To join and be joined.
What difference if it is a tribe of black clouds,
a v of geese, a swarm of waves,
what earthly difference.

Some Time in Truro

I almost wake you.
It's not that you need to see the billowing
of the white muslin curtains, how they seem
another, more tender, quiet form of surf,
since making love through most of the night,
we billowed and curled
to and away from each other
in our own tides of want and rest.
And it is not because this is our first morning
ever intertwined
and you need to see how the sky remains cloudless,
the sun draped along the ocean surface,
and it's not that you need to see
that you can sleep your effortless sleep
next to me.

I almost wake you
because I want a retelling,
how last evening, sitting on the beach,
the darkness falling around us like tapestries,
how this "might have been"
simply and finally began
in the gesture of an offered sweater.

I don't wake you
because you may be dreaming

and I may be in it,
and when you wake
you will slide your head onto my chest
and tell me your dream.
We will dive together into it
and match our strokes,
trim through the water and careless
of any destination.

Raspberry Jam

to step lightly, lightly —
— James Wright

Breakfast shimmers.

Such a red, concentrated
essence of raspberry
so I see a clearing,
a butterfly
and those bushes, their berries
soft and scarlet as a cape of light.

I am near the point
where my joy explodes
into a profusion of breezes,
each one redolent with fruit,
each one instructed
to find someone from my past
who was then or is now unhappy
and kiss them out of it.

Letter from a Vacation

A mourning dove, with his too small head,
pecks the lawn for seeds.
Today I see him
as a precise, individual thing
where before he was a category,
maybe one less daily blindness.
Everything else is quiet
and as we hoped, calm surf, fresh corn,
buying fish just off the boats, real
tomatoes, enough sleep.

Yesterday it poured,
though late in the afternoon it began to clear
so I walked to the beach.
The sky stood split open, rampaging
fists of black clouds, new rolling whites,
the sun momentarily spinning out from behind
so that the light struck down
in bands of yellow, black, and grey
like a beaded curtain
I could put my hand right through
and the sea sucked and squeezed the light
into a silver patina
as it roiled over and over on itself,
like an absolute obsession.

The scene sped past all its checkpoints,
and I sensed that all the engines,
all the secret works were becoming visible.
I felt enormous,
like Tolstoy.

Yet this morning, I am happy to have grown
back toward myself,
my smaller things, a glass of juice,
the newspaper, this dove
working my lawn with purpose
but without ambition.
You know how it is.

In the Car, Evening

How much luck got me here,
my younger son napping against me,
my older, up the path, fishing
and near, framed in the car window,
a small hummock of sunlit dune.

Where the last light falls,
everything glows with the white fire
of cleanliness, the bold grace of edge,
even a patch of stinkweed
stands redeemed in the light.

And soon will come those few moments
of purple, that checkpoint
of rods and cones
where the world hovers
waiting its pass to the night.

And he will sleep against me,
and he will bring in his fish,
and the birds will cease their wheeling,
the wind will quiet
and the tide come in.

Mozart

CLARINET QUINTET IN A MAJOR, K. 581

For his great friend, the clarinetist
Stadler, nothing less than transmutation.
The violins become companies
of handsome lieutenants of the guard,
the cello, smooth wooden carriage wheels
over the bridges' stone arches,
a grace of circles. But it is the clarinet
with its beautiful manners
that expands in each successive phrase
the alchemies of elegance,
the sheerest veils of yellow tulle,
the white glazes of porcelain into the still,
dappled water of woodwind sound.

And what is it that elegance
cannot express?

Listen to this sadness as it curls
out of the strings of the Larghetto,
a stream between the placid plane trees
in an afternoon so still that the heart
hears clearly the voices it can never have

and we grow, quietly and slowly,
fuller for this sadness
which fits into a world that can mesh it
with the ascending voice of the clarinet,
that wand for when we dream of
how to take the world into our hands
and refashion it.

STRING QUINTET IN G MINOR, K. 516

Whichever hour it is, it is late.
He steadies his fingers against the cool
glass of the window, while the darkness
pushes the clock forward and forward.
His waiting is indiscriminate.
The square below is as black
as if the bottom of the sea
had come to Vienna.

And this is exact music,
without haze, without shadow:
emptiness put through
a prism of strings, registering
each dark and darkening wave
as it reaches the heart.

Listen to its clarity, the grace
that asks us not to light the darkness
but to enter and absorb it, to know
in each note how cold we may grow,
how barren the soul will find itself
on this night that will always come,
to learn in the precision
of the violins and cello, of the two violas
that harmony and beauty
release us only from the fear.

Adagio from the Serenade for Thirteen Wind Instruments, K. 361

Sadness is the first moon of beauty
and its light falls from the oboe.

A garden, perfumed
with stillness. The lights
from the paper lanterns flicker
over the brocade of flowers,
the stars blaze like palace windows.

Yet the world goes steadily from us,
from our heart and its moonlit pictures
though the clarinets and oboes,
the bassoons and bassethorns
say this loss is delicate,
calm, strands of curling smoke.

Overture from Cosi Fan Tutte, K. 588:
An Imaginary Letter

Dearest, most beloved little wife,

This morning I finished the opera. How much
I love writing the overtures, they are
the most wonderful candy we save for last.
Today, as I wrote, I imagined
the audience entering the theatre,
gossiping, preening, gossiping,
the servants crossing the corridors
with notes for the new lovers, would-be lovers
or the old and discarded lovers
(shall I ask Da Ponte for a buffa
set entirely in an opera house?)
and then my orchestra begins.
What a game the overture is, what I choose
to announce and what I choose to hide.
Here are the soldiers, there the coquettes
and then this little phrase, how important
could it be, that will become cosi fan tutte.
Haydn is coming to rehearsal tomorrow.

And you, my little bird bathing at Baden,
where have I hidden you in this music?
Will you be able to guess?
Have I put you in the winds, those little
running phrases, so quick, light,

I remember how irresistible you are to me
always as you dress, will you find your satins
rustling in their flutter?
Or is that your pitch in the nervous strings
when I come home without the money
for the bills? Or are you in the timpani,
how deeply you gasp when I touch you
there.

I have finished and am happy today.
But how little we have been together lately.
Prague, Salzburg, Munich, brittle Dresden,
those running flutes are really the phrases
of our distance, of longings that rise
so fast in me I can cover them only
with the lightest of jokes.
And then there are days without you, those cellos,
when I feel I am the holes of my lace.

Ah, but this is a buffa and you return to me
soon. Lovers reunited, wiser for their pain.
Puchberg is come to take me to dinner. I kiss you
and squeeze you 1095060437082 times and am ever
your most faithful husband and friend.

W. A. Mozart

Rondo from the Violin Concerto #5 in A Major, K. 219, The Turkish

Let us forsake the evening, the soft
breeze and the elegant, sculpted walks,
the flowers pouring their cups of scent,
the casual and pregnant nod to the lady
in blue, the Italian wife, all those
infinite truths of the rondo.

And let the Turks come, let them invade
the concertos and then the cities,
let their scimitars flash, dervishes
whirl, all their green crescent crimes.
Let us invoke them, wild muses
of our double time, squadrons of the comic,
these janissary dreams out of our
private easts.

But as a gesture to an old friend,
let the rondo reassemble itself
for one last moment, one last time,
though now a bit touched, a bit crazy.

An Answer

My answer: listen to Mozart
    (which is to say)
            that grief is not simply erosive
              wind and rain scouring channels through a heart
      nor is it glacial
        depositing moraines of tears and longing
      but, with the curious reverse english
          that is each thing human, is bedrock
(the granite of his quintets)
            fused by the heats of harmony and order
                    into grace
             the achievements of metamorphics.

Remember, light *shines.*
If we look toward it, all around the source
is obscured, vanished with the eye's inability
(and the heart's as well) to open and close
           faster than glow

      so this scene of sea and sky and sea,
        lit with that particular cleansing brilliance
          of late afternoon late summer
      the sense of gift arriving with each wave
             deep color and deep sound

and to doom this for its
irrelevance to suffering
    of a world dying in every stage
                in every place
    of children experienced in every pain
    of each agony a place name
    each ache a fever, each fever a plague
      (you see, the list is always available)

is to insist on what they taught you:
that salvation is so rare
        it demands a God's suffering,
          nails and blood and the balm of darkness

    while silly fool that I am, amid the shining light,
    I see the answer to your question:
        where is the heart this lung-wide ocean feeds?

            inside your chest.

ACKNOWLEDGMENTS

Some of the poems in this book, often in slightly different versions, first appeared or are scheduled to appear in the following publications:

American Letters and Commentary: "The Kabbalist's Pencil"; *American Poetry Review:* "The Spanish Poets," "Hands," "Montauk and the World Revealed through the Magic of New Orleans"; *The Big Spoon:* "Overture from Cosi Fan Tutte, K.588: An Imaginary Letter," "Clarinet Quintet in A Major, K. 581"; *Columbia:* "Sagaponack"; *The Georgia Review:* "String Quintet in G Minor, K. 516"; *The Gettysburg Review:* "The Vibrant Archipelagoes"; *The Paris Review:* "This Web" (originally titled "To Aleksander Wat"), "Matisse in the Rotogravure: The Cutouts"; *Poetry:* "Rondo from the Violin Concerto #5 in A Major, K. 219, The Turkish"; *Prairie Schooner:* "The Doctor," "Early Morning Song"; *Slow Loris Reader:* "Strange Town"; *Sou'wester:* "The Adoration"; *The Threepenny Review:* "A Poem About Furniture"; *Twice:* "Reshapings," "Insomnia," "The Poem," "Turning Fifty"

I would like to thank Donald Sheehan and the Frost Place for helping me to return to my poetry, and to all my friends there for their interest and their care, but especially to Didi Goldenhar, Baron Wormser, David Keller, Peter Wood, Jeanne Marie Beaumont, Lisa Rhoades, Allison Funk, and Julie Agoos for their critical acuity and their faith. Also to Joan Cusack Handler for her enthusiasm, her vision and her absolute dedication to this book, and to Molly Peacock for her indispensable insight.